# Invisible Lines

# Invisible Lines

Poems by

Miriam Manglani

© 2025 Miriam Manglani. All rights reserved.
This material may not be reproduced in any form, published,
reprinted, recorded, performed, broadcast,
rewritten, or redistributed without
the explicit permission of Miriam Manglani.
All such actions are strictly prohibited by law.

Cover image by Florence Manglani
Author photo by Liz McEachern Hall

ISBN: 978-1-63980-740-6
Library of Congress Control Number: 2025938082

Kelsay Books
502 South 1040 East, A-119
American Fork, Utah 84003
Kelsaybooks.com

# Acknowledgments

Sincere gratitude goes out to the following publications where these poems or earlier versions of them first appeared:

*The Bloom:* "Pears in the Snack Bowl"
*Canyon Voices*: "My Granddaughter Sits on My Lap"
*Cerasus Magazine:* "Natural Highlights," "Visitation in a Small Urban Yard" as "Rabbit in a Small City Front Yard"
*Coneflower Cafe:* "Lost Luggage," "First Words," "I Wish I Could Stretch the Night Out"
*Fresh Words:* "Her Cooking Symphony" as "Musical Cook," "My Hollow," "Palimpsest"
*Glacial Hills Review:* "Their Shared Air" as "My Sons Whistling," "Artifacts" as "That Photo"
*Glimpse:* "They've Come"
*Ibbetson St. Press:* "Women's College Reunion"
*Lothlorian Poetry Journal:* "Falling to New Heights," "Ode to My Breasts," "My Father's Yahrzeit"
*The Marbled Sigh:* "His Reflection"
*Medical Literary Messenger:* "The Mommy Within"
*OneArt:* "First Letter Home from Camp," "Depression" as "The Depression"
*Ordinary Wonders:* "Challah," "Ever Since That Day He's Been Carrying Her" as "Carrying Her," "Saving a Life"
*Poetry Quarterly:* "Missing My Twin Baby Boys"
*Poetry of Science:* "Makince's Quantum World," "Her Volcano"
*Prospectus:* "We Dug Like Miners" as "Digging with Pails"
*Red Eft Review:* "Artifacts" as "Video Tapes"
*Round Table Literary Journal:* "My Final Goodbye" as "When I Am Dead
*Rushing Thru the Dark:* "Stones for His Grave"
*Sparks of Calliope:* "To My Father Who Immigrated to America," "Homeless Village," "Paper Weight," "Metal on Bone," "Their Music," "Sewing Memories"

*Spell Jar Press:* "Let's Pluck the Moon from the Sky Tonight,"
  "Silver Eye," "The Moon Is Pregnant with Dreams"
*The Stillwater Review:* "Our Escape" as "Camping"
*Synkroniciti:* "House Plant"
*Village Square:* "The Never-Was-But-Could-Have-Been,"
  "Invisible Lines," "The Stranger," "Dinosaur Bones" as "The Dinosaur Will Get a Makeover"
*Vita Brevis:* "Our Pine"
*Wheelsong Poetry Anthology 2:* "Low Tide"
*Writer Shed Press:* "The Tooth"

\*\*\*

"They've Come" was a finalist for The Beals Prize for poetry in 2023.

"Pears in the Snack Bowl" won honorable mention in the 2024 Kelseyville Pear Festival Poetry Contest.

\*\*\*

This book is a culmination of years of work brought to fruition by the contributions of many. A momentous thank you to all who have helped me in my journey to publication.

To Writer's Village University that provided the support my writing needed to flourish through their online courses and supportive community.

To my poetry peers at Writer's Village University, specifically Fran Schumer, Enza Caratozzolo, Malkeet Kaur, Maggie Fieland, Brigitte Whiting, and Glennis Hobbs for their insightful feeedback on my work.

To Glenn Lyvers who edited and published my first chapbook, "Ordinary Wonders."

To John Sibley Williams who edited my poetry book manuscript and encouraged me to add depth to my writing.

To the 2020 global pandemic that gave me the inspiration and time to return to poetry writing after a more than twenty-year hiatus.

To my family who gave me the space and time I needed to write.

To my mother-in-law who encouraged me to write and saw the strength of my words.

To my mother who has always been proud of my writing.

To my husband who loves me unconditionally even though he does not care for poetry and would rather see me doing something other than writing.

Finally, to my father who was an inspiration and appears in many pages of this book.

This book is dedicated to my beautiful family.

# Contents

I. Still Give Rise

| | |
|---|---|
| To My Father Who Immigrated to America | 17 |
| Challah | 19 |
| Swimming in the Sun | 20 |
| Invisible Lines | 21 |
| The Tooth | 23 |
| First Words | 24 |
| Missing My Twin Baby Boys | 26 |
| First Letter Home from Camp | 28 |
| Dinosaur Bones | 29 |
| They've Come | 30 |
| Their Shared Air | 31 |
| My Final Goodbye | 32 |
| Artifacts | 33 |
| The Mommy Within | 35 |
| Her Cooking Symphony | 37 |
| Metal on Bone | 38 |
| The Stranger | 39 |
| The Never-Was-But-Could-Have-Been | 40 |
| Stones for His Grave | 41 |
| My Father's Yahrzeit | 42 |
| Depression | 43 |
| His Reflection | 44 |
| Paper Weight | 45 |
| Clinic Shootings | 46 |
| Sewing Memories | 48 |

II. Into the Sacred

| | |
|---|---|
| Visitation in a Small Urban Yard | 53 |
| We Dug Like Miners | 54 |
| Our Escape | 55 |

| | |
|---|---|
| Our Pine | 56 |
| House on Lee Street | 57 |
| House Plant | 58 |
| I Wish I Could Stretch the Night Out | 59 |
| Let's Pluck the Moon from the Sky Tonight | 60 |
| The Moon Is Pregnant with Dreams | 61 |
| Silver Eye | 62 |
| Let's Take Down the Sun | 63 |
| Low Tide | 64 |

## III. Temporary Paradise

| | |
|---|---|
| Palimpsest | 67 |
| Falling to New Heights | 68 |
| This Body of Mine | 70 |
| Ode to My Breasts | 71 |
| Natural Highlights | 72 |
| Homeless Village | 73 |
| Lost Luggage | 74 |
| Lucid Dreaming | 76 |
| My Hollow | 77 |
| Her Painted Smile | 78 |
| Saving a Life | 79 |
| Ever Since That Day He's Been Carrying Her | 80 |
| Women's College Reunion | 81 |
| Pears in the Snack Bowl | 82 |
| My Granddaughter Sits on My Lap | 83 |
| Their Music | 84 |
| Her Volcano | 86 |
| Makinde's Quantum World | 87 |

I. Still Give Rise

# To My Father Who Immigrated to America

How scared you must have been
leaving your native Egypt,
the only home you knew,
        alone,
leaving your parents,
your seven siblings,
your friends,
by boat at twenty-two
with only sixteen dollars in your pocket,
driven out by antisemitism,
the gang of Arabs
who beat you,
almost killed you for being Jewish.

Perhaps you saw glints of the lives
you would create and change
in the waters
of that gleaming Mediterranean
you crossed—

Perhaps you saw in France
beneath the layers of soot
on the copper chimneys you cleaned,
for one long dirty year—
glimmers of the trail you turned years later
as a renowned OB/GYN,
reflections of the many women you saved
who regarded you as a quiet hero,
facets of the worlds you helped create
for your future wife, children,
and your grandchildren
who only know your cold grave.

When you stepped on American soil,
did you feel the rush of wind
from the golden doors
of opportunity swinging wide open?

Perhaps you saw and felt none
of those wondrous things,
but you still gave rise to them all.

# Challah

When I get to that part
where my hands are holding
and kneading the soft, warm dough,
it's like cradling a baby,
soft and lukewarm,
and all the weighing,
      measuring,
      mixing,
      kneading,
and patiently waiting for it to rise
           was worth it
to get to that luscious, simple dough
alive and bubbling with air
that I braid like my daughter's hair.

# Swimming in the Sun

After several failures,
this one's heartbeat lit up
the monitor like a full moon.
At 12 weeks, the monitor was dark.

We had so many plans.

Weeks later in a dream
you were at the water's edge
and dove head-first into the sunset.

You drank in the oranges,
floated in the reds,
bathed in the shimmering yellows,
and wrapped yourself in its molten golds.

You glowed,
you burned gloriously,
as your shadow melted into the horizon
and sunk with the sun.

When you woke up,
enveloped in my arms,
you rose with the new sun,
like our future crowning newborn.
You shined within
strong,
unrelenting,

and ready to try again.

# Invisible Lines

When I first saw them
on the ultrasound screen,
    worlds unfurled
in the black and white grainy images,
like shapes in a Kaleidoscope.

Invisible lines formed,
bonding me to each,
strengthened by rhythmic sounds of drums
       played under the sea
that filled every corner of the sterile exam room.

My worries about their survival
calmed by their heart beats.

I rubbed bulging limbs,
sang to them in the shower,
imagined them reading my mind,
tasting my craves:
rock hard sour nectarines,
and vanilla ice cream.

Birth's aftermath altered connections,
I turned into an empty egg shell,
cracked and broken with exhaustion.
The invisible lines turned to shadows.

Months later,

I watched one fall asleep as he melted
into me with his warmth.
His eyes shaped like almonds
with their long, curly lashes

interlocked like clamshells.
I touched his translucent finger nails,
his thin lips
with drops of milk in their creases.

I looked at the other in his bassinet.
His lashes, black wings ready to fly.
His dark eyes, black holes against
his milky white complexion
drawing in our shared line.

I was full with them again.
The invisible lines turned to soft ropes,
tugged on my insides,
wrapped around me,
pulling me into our babies' newfound worlds.

# The Tooth

She anxiously awaits
her tooth's crowning glory,
a mountain peaking through
        clouds above.

The money she'll find
will make her smile
        when she wakes

with a bone of her childhood
buried like treasure under her head.

# First Words

She stands in front of her plastic kitchen,
looks up at me with simmering eyes,
holds her pretend spoon—

*Spatchelula!*

So I picture a dancing spatula
with flowing skirt,
multicolored leis,
face with big red lips,
and lashes as long as hers.

He plays with his fire engine,
it's wheels spinning like his raindow top—

*Furdenden*

I imagine a furry animal
clomping on cylinder shaped legs
muttering "den den"
with its cavernous mouth.

She points to the vacuum cleaner
that terrifies her, says

*Gaboon*

I picture a baboon
with long vacuuming snout,
steam teaming from his nostrils,
making an "umm ummm" sound

He used to say

    *Beba*

Years later, I still don't know what it represents
but it always made him smile.

Their words,
their weight,
expands the world with possibility
so much larger than them.

# Missing My Twin Baby Boys

Today I laid in bed with one,
he came willingly,
like a bird to seed into my needy arms.

I stroked his thick hair,
his tiny seven-year old belly,
and remembered a time
when I didn't yearn for these moments
and would draw energy
from long, snuggly naps with my babies.

A time when I was a slave to the bottles
washing them around the clock,
filling them with precisely measured
portions of powdered formula,
something I could control—
unlike the shit-overflowing diapers,
the spit-up,
the repeated wake-ups—
I could arrange our night-time arsenal
in even rows on a tray,
like missiles on a launch pad,
their glass clinking as I carried them upstairs.

A time when I needed them too,
to dis-engorge *my* painful swollen breasts,
hard as grenades,
*theirs* until they stopped wanting them.

A time when we claimed the wee hours of morning,
poked our tired heads
through its thick blanket of silence.

A time when their screaming and crying
raked through our raw nerves
reaching unbelievable decibels,
when all twelve of our pacifiers were hiding
like delinquent children,
and we were too tired
to even think of looking for them.

A time when I woke to their babbling,
sometimes unsure if I was still dreaming,
the beautiful nonsense sounds
like the flow of rain down our windows.

# First Letter Home from Camp

After two long weeks,
his first letter finally arrives.

I wrap my hands around it.
Paper he touched
with warm tiny hands,
envelope he sealed shut,
little face puckering like a raisin
with the sour taste of glue.

I tear it open
to read a note
in his nine-year-old attempt at handwriting.
Just one sentence.
"I must tell you my fan broke."

# Dinosaur Bones

She talks of makeovers with friends,
using contour sticks and beauty blenders,
making TikToks with dance moves
called the "Woah" and "Say So."

She dances next to me,
her lithe, thin body
moving like a ribbon in the wind
in a way mine never could.

We talk of doing my makeup,
fitting my bulky thighs in skinny jeans
and buying me a trendy baggy sweater
so she isn't embarrassed
by my grungy sweats.

She wants to "draw" my eyebrows.
"I have eyebrows," I reply.
She giggles and explains
what "drawing eyebrows" really means.

"I'm a dinosaur," I say.
She looks at me puzzled.
"No you're not. Dinosaurs are cool."

My mind fast forwards years ahead.
Will she be hip,
or will her children unearth
my dinosaur bones?

# They've Come

The day of their return from camp has come.
Bye-bye sweet silence.
Bye-bye lazy late afternoons.

They've come with their dirt,
their smelliness,
duffle bags packed with dirty laundry
and stow-away bugs—
a washing and folding marathon awaits.

They've come with their smiles and laughter,
hungry bellies,
their father's brown, soupy wide eyes
and delicate lashes.

They've come with their wonder,
questions, stories, and loud excited voices,
their thick hair overgrown,
like matted, shaggy rugs.

They've come with their hugs and kisses
I haven't felt in weeks.

# Their Shared Air

My son is a beautiful whistler,
often unaware he's whistling,
his notes as natural as breathing.

If I listen closely and close my eyes,
I can hear my dead father's song

as if my son was blowing
the same decades old air
from his young lungs,

kissing it warmly with his
grandfather's thin lips,
fanning decades together.

# My Final Goodbye

When I am dead, my dear,
you must kiss our children
every night before bed
as if your lips were mine.

Please start lifting weights—
so when you hug our children every night
they will feel both our arms hugging them as one.

You must remind them
I am in the very air they breathe,
the things they touch and are touched by,
and their tiny hearts
opening wider every day.

And please don't forget
I'm with you too—
in your shadow and reflection,
your image cast on the world.

Talk to me as I will be lonely without you.
I'll hear you with invisible ears,
see you with invisible eyes.
I'll be in the spaces between
the leaves and grains of sand,
between the waves that lap the shore
and the endless expanse
beyond.

# Artifacts

1. Videos

I found them in a dusty bag in my mom's attic
buried under a stack of board games,
a box of pens,
and a pile of vinyl records.

So unassuming
in their black plastic cases
one would never suspect they had captured
precious pieces of the past—
my father's final words to his children
staring into the camera with his shiny soulful eyes.

Encoded in flimsy tape,
my mom's pre-stroke voice,
the one I couldn't summon in my head
when I needed to hear it most.
Now I can drink it like a potion
to conjure up mommy
preserved like a fine artifact.


2. Photo

There is something about that photo.
Could it be that her eye shadow
matches the color of the sky?
Or its uncommon graininess,
revealing its status as an artifact of the past?
Perhaps it's her smiling at something off camera,
her head cocked to the side,

and how she's looking at it
so you can't see straight into her eyes
that leaves you wondering what has her attention.
Perhaps it's the way she's hunched over
with her fingers fanned out on her thighs
as if they were the bones of wings ready to fly.

But it's none of those things.
It's a photo of my mother
before her stroke
when even the dark sky
seemed to light up when she smiled.

# The Mommy Within

In her hospital room, she turned
into another person today,
all her color drained
like watermelon flesh sucked dry.

A week after her stroke,
the word "gooood,"
eked out of her mouth,
a balloon deflating.

Weeks later, without
an arm bracing her waist,
she walked again,
shuffling like a toddler.

I read to her,
remembering how mommy read to me,
and she learned to read,
again,
her mouth stiff,
as if caught in a fishing line,
struggling to utter basic sounds.

"Whatever happens, we need happy," she said.

Before her stoke, her smile was electric.
Years later, reticent and reserved,
her rare grins, hardly arresting.

Once thin, she exists in the mold of her old body—
in clothing too tight,
gait wobbly in heels,
hair falling out of clips.

There hides the former mommy,
the dolled up one,
with thick, shiny curls that boing.

The one I see in glints,
in her eyes or the memories she ignites—
small flecks of quartz in stone.
Mommy never stays.

"Whatever happens, we need happy," I remind myself.

# Her Cooking Symphony

She plays her cookware,
instruments of her domestic domain,
spatulas, spoons, pots—
dances across the kitchen floor,
from stove to oven
to oven again,
Arabic music blares—

She creates flavor notes,
dash of cumin,
teaspoon of coriander,
clove of garlic,
pinch of posterity,
sprinkling of motherhood,
slice of her homeland,
coalesce into a symphony of exotic aromas
wafting from open windows
of her American décor home.

Egyptian foods her mom cooked for her—
passed down from generations—
masterpieces enjoyed in minutes
sing timeless songs.

# Metal on Bone

When my mom's friend Arthritis
brewed a storm in her knees,
flushing the toilet made her fall.

She was found crumpled
on her bathroom floor
like balled up toilet paper.

X-rays and scans unearthed
her injury—a break in her femur.

She has metal in her now—
her organic existence compromised
with rods and screws that will join her
in her earthy grave.

Her family has faith in the skill of surgeons,
the fidelity of screws,
the strength of metal,
her mettle,
for the long journey to recovery
that stretches barren before her.

They pray she will be able to walk again,
metal on bone,
bone with mettle.

# The Stranger

You were always quiet
but still grew quieter.
There were other small signs—
you opened the fridge with your left hand,
parked forward in the garage
when you usually backed in.

Death worked you hard.

You lost the ability to converse
before clinging to a few basic words.
"No" and "yes" were your life rafts.
But eventually even they left you
                       drowning . . .

in thick frustration that blazed red through your face
and singed the air around you.

You stared at your reflection in the mirror,
unable to recognize it, scared of the stranger
who stared back with the dull eyes of a dead fish.

You didn't recognize me
and lost the ability to walk,
swearing in your native Arabic at your dead legs.

Two years later, pneumonia gripped your lungs
and your breathing stopped,
but you had died several deaths before,
each one never grieved.

# The Never-Was-But-Could-Have-Been

I never doubted that he loved me
even after he died from dementia—
There were tight hugs scented with aftershave,
stubble rubs prickled my skin,
and there were gifts of toys, puzzles, and bikes.

But it was his attention
I never stopped wanting,
out of reach like a prized toy
in a locked box on the top shelf.
Not even he had the key.

His words were few.
Talk about the weather, Aesop's Fables,
obscure riddles—
passed through my young mind
like water through a sieve.

He had infinite patience for his patients
but not for me
who could never move fast enough
or "stop doing the crazies!"

I wondered about a "normal"
paternal relationship
just like I wondered about sex.

The never-was-but-could-have-been
wakes and aches at the sight
of a father and daughter together
like a bad knee in the rain.

# Stones for His Grave

He never moves.
Sometimes dressed in thick grass.
Today, glittering with ice and snow.

I talk to the still, chilly air
hoping there is something of him
left there to hear me.

I pry a stone loose from the earth
with an icy stick
and leave it on his grave
next to the purple one
left by the grandson he never met.

"Daddy, this stone is for you," I say
hoping he's admiring it now.

I remember how he enjoyed
rocks, coins, shells—
the simple things in life,
a walk on the beach,
eating ice cream.

The stone is tiny
compared to the one in my gut
that sinks lower and lower,
its descent
announced by the squawking geese
taking flight behind me.

# My Father's Yahrzeit

Every year I visit you.
I search for you in a forest of stones.
I talk to you, but you are soundless.
Lichen has swallowed over your name.

I search for you in a graveyard.
Your stone feels cold.
Lichen swallows your name.
You've left a hole in me.

Your stone is cold.
I feel the shadow of your presence.
The hole you left is healing.
I miss your eyes, little pools of light.

I search for the shadow of your presence.
I see you in my smile.
I miss the lost spirit in your eyes.
The sun doesn't feel as warm as it used to.

I have your crescent moon smile.
I miss knowing you would always be there for me.
The sun keeps getting colder.
I miss hearing your old-fashioned funny sayings.

I miss knowing you would be there for me.
I talk to you, but you can't reply.
I miss hearing your old-fashioned sayings.
Every year I miss you more.

# Depression

Daddy, when I visited your grave this year,
fifteen years after your death,
I noticed the ground had sunk,
the length of the depression
about the length of your coffin.

Your burial, like all things eventually will,
entered an advanced state of decomposition.

Your tombstone, crawling with lichen.
Your coffin, disintegrated.

Below me, only dirt cradled your bones.
The air your body had in its
former wooden home—gone.
And all my tangled roots—decaying.

# His Reflection

Parts of my father slip away gradually,
the loss of his core being
a punch to the gut
the day he didn't know who I was
or even who he was.

I caught his familiar
glinting eyes in the mirror
and know he's in me,
in my DNA,
in the blood circulating in me,
part of him
alive in me,
keeping me alive,
like he's become
part earth.

# Paper Weight

They float in a perfect cube of clear resin,
a set of US mint coins from 1994.
He kept it on a dusty shelf
in his doctor's office, next to the penguin
wearing a beret I sculpted for him.

We would take family trips to flea markets
so he could look for coins,
dollars, half dollars, nickels, pennies, silver, copper—

he felt their weight and contours
in his deft surgeon hands,
the coins preserved, frozen in time,
memories of a time long gone,

a reminder and remainder of him
and the unquantifiable weight of his loss.

# Clinic Shootings

*On Dec 30, 1994, John Salvi entered two abortion clinics
in Brookline, Massachusetts killing two and injuring five.*

She knew her father performed abortions,
the Sunday morning trips to the flea market
to avoid the pro-life protesters
outside their driveway circling
like a mass of ants—
each thrusting a picket sign in the air,
burning with words of hate for him.

Weeks prior,
there were threatening phone calls,
their hostile voices trapped in her head,
raging with the guttural sounds of rabid animals.

Weeks prior,
their porch walls bled
from floor to ceiling with hate graffiti,
she could feel the black pointy letters
crawling like insect legs on her skin.

That day her father came home
with sirens blaring—
a serpentine succession
of police and FBI vehicles parked
haphazardly in the backyard.

That day she learned
he held his clinic's dying receptionist
in his arms,
and tried to stop the bleeding
from a gunshot wound in her neck
using a Kotex pad.

That day she saw for the first time
his invisible cape—
risking his life to give women
the right to choose—
choose to keep their wings.

## Sewing Memories

She sews the tapestry of her life
with tender threads of time.

Memories faded like laundry hanging
out to dry in the sun
are stitched together piece by piece.

Red fabric with the "S" Superman logo—
from the T-shirt she lived in
when she was five.

Rough black fabric—
prickly feel of her father's stubble
when he hugged her goodnight.

Green shimmery fabric—
color of ocean waves
she rode every summer as a child.

Yellow fabric—
color that danced into her mind
when she smelled her mom's Egyptian soup.

Rainbow fabric—
for the wistfulness she felt
when dancing to "their song"
"Forever Young" on her wedding day.

Black fabric—
color of her daughter's
long lashes.

Burp cloth fabric—
a reminder of the sleepless nights
she spent nursing twin boys.

Jean fabric—
torn to save her mom's life
when she had a stroke.

She sees them all now,
her memories threaded together.

She feels them all now,
slide through her fingers.

# II. Into the Sacred

# Visitation in a Small Urban Yard

The rabbit's brown-marble-eyes
        transfix me,
sharing a moment of quiet twilight.

Beneath a leafy tree, where time moves
slower than the pressing darkness,
slower than the falling leaves,

slower than ghosted breezes rustling its fur,
calming my worries
like soft music before sleep.

Its silver whiskers arch like a crescent moon,
its pink ears, translucent like wet flower petals.

Let me be a hair on its soft back
riding into sacred, quiet woods.

# We Dug Like Miners

uncovering
        seashells,
                crab claws,
last year's broken peach pits.
The sound of our pails
fell in sync with the ocean's
wavy pulse,
        *digging,*
                *digging,*
as we hauled a childhood of buckets,
the teaming sky above
swimming in a soup of seaweed,
                driftwood,
small polished pebbles.

We spilled the sky on the sand,
        letting it seep in
and solidify like concrete
that clung to our bodies,
making its way
into our bathing suits and hair,
pressing itself annoyingly
into tender, tiny spaces.

We became the other flotsam
it had swallowed up,
burying ourselves,
our heads sticking out—
how brazen we were
to dig a place for ourselves in the world,
with just water and a small plastic pail.

# Our Escape

We left rat infested streets,
smog draped sky,
urine-soaked subways,
and our nine to fives
for the woods.

We ate fried babka, s'mores, eggs with salsa—
cooked in the thinnest of pans
with a propane blow torch
under shedding pines and drenching sun.

We swam in bone cold water
after a day in the heat,
caught the running river in our hair.

Night's dark face
blanketed us before sleep
and we drowned wide-eyed in cricket thrum.

We returned to the bowels
of our former lives,
memories of our trip
kindling in our dark woods.

# Our Pine

Beneath its maternal arms,
we crouched on dry needle beds
lit with rays of filtered sun,
inhaled the crisp scent of divine pine.

We invented our own worlds
in its cool shade.
Worlds that waited patiently
for us to return,
arrested worlds, protected,
under snow and ice
where sticks became wands
mud piles became dragons,
circles of rocks, castles,
and we become princesses and kings
with wreathes of pine cones,
rulers of our under-pine kingdom.

We climbed the length of its body,
oozing with sticky sap
with our ropey arms and legs,

and mud-slicked sneakers
to heights that made our bellies quiver,
and our legs shake in frightful delight,
our real world, small and hollow, below.

# House on Lee Street

I search for it online like a stalker,
secretly wish it would go up for sale
so I can walk through it again.

Would I hear the voice of my father
long dead, echoing in its halls?
The clomp, clomp clomp,
of his feet as he ran to his red
office phone ringing
for a medical emergency?
The voice of my mother
frothing with laughter,
the sound of her nimble steps
on the tiled kitchen floor?

Would I smell mom's cooking
wafting like sea breeze?
See the little girl perched in the tree
by the driveway daydreaming
to the thrum of traffic?

I stare longingly at its brick exterior,
yet know what was once home
is now just another address.

# House Plant

It's always been here
on the side table,
long after you left me for someone else,
growing leafier as I tend to it—
its branches spilling over
our edges—
entwining—the way we
used to when we slept together,
my legs wrapped securely around yours,
our desires gushing like hot summer rain,
as we grew into each other,
anchored our merged roots
into the soil of our shared world.

# I Wish I Could Stretch the Night Out

like taffy so we could lay in it longer,
a hammock for our naked bodies,
nestled crescent moons.

As the sun rises and spreads
its fingers of light
over a sleepy night,
thoughts of you leaving me
and the warmth we've created
darken the morning.

I run my hands through
your hair where wild fires burn,
stroke your warm dark cheek,
dive into the green pools of your gaze
where I drift in waves.

Between waking and dreaming,
I pull a corner of the night,
stretching it out,
to cradle the infinite stars we create.

# Let's Pluck the Moon from the Sky Tonight

It's ready,
perfectly ripe and round.

We'll cut her into wedges,
serve her on a silver platter
to match her reflection
and season her
with lemon juice and stardust.

Crisp, dry, and sweet,
we'll wash her down
with a glass of wine.

When we're done,
we'll be suffused with her,
satiated to our cores—
every part of us glowing
with a single night of peace.

# The Moon Is Pregnant with Dreams

Teeming in her warm womb
like schools of fish.

They gush out of her into darkness
as she wanes—
silvery wisps sailing through space
down to earth

ignite our souls with desire.

# Silver Eye

She is the silver eye
of the night's sky,
slivered, halved, or fully awake,
still as a frigid lake.

She has a penetrating stare
with gray-blue glare,
makes us wanderlust,
yearn to find our stardust.

A seed for dreams
that grow when she gleams
in the womb of the night
she is love's waning light,
our passionate insight.

# Let's Take Down the Sun

We'll roll him to a juicer
and squeeze him dry,
his red liquid gushing out—
swirling with streaks of yellow and orange.

We'll drink him for breakfast
with a side of eggs sunny-side up,
and suck orange wedges to mask
his sulfurous flavor.

We'll radiate his red and orange glow,
every part of us coursing with the fires of his world.

# Low Tide

Its naked bed stretches for miles,
pocked with murky, stray pools
and lives left behind.

The sea of you,
once warm and so near,
is now barely visible in
the horizon of my mind.

Unlike the tide, you will
never return to my shores,
where memories still puddle.

I reach for you, as ever you recede
into uncharted depths.

III. Temporary Paradise

# Palimpsest

*Something reused or altered
but still bearing visible traces
of its earlier form.*

I am a palimpsest—
scared with the past,
wounds beneath
semi-transparent layers of life
reveal memories
that pit my insides
like daggers.

My eyes shine and mist,
lips crescent and quiver,
hands tremble, legs buckle.

Peel me, peel me,
like an onion
one layer at a time,
to reach the pure core of me
vulnerable and so shiny
it could burn holes in your eyes.

## Falling to New Heights

I watched myself fall
off the wobbly dock—
my friends pushed
me into the cold lake,
steely as a nickel.

Fear swam in my eyes,
my hands flailed,
my legs froze,
my hair fluttered in the air.

One second felt like too many lifetimes—
to break the still surface of the lake.

The electric shock of the cold water.
My being returned to its home.

I had to grab their two-timing hands
to climb back onto the dock,
my heavy winter clothing
weighed down with lake water.

The anger that should have lit me like kindling—
breezed through,
awe took its place.
I felt weightless,
like I could fly.

The world was sharper,
lighter,
charged with divine current—
it surged in me,
nerves open and alive,
the feeling of being more
than mere flesh and bones.

## This Body of Mine

was tan, muscular,
sung with the fire of youth,
reached for the highest monkey bars.

coursed with fiery hormones—
sprouted breasts, hair, curves,
and spouted rivers of raging blood.

raced, rowed, hit, and kicked—
grew faster and stronger,
invincible like Superman.

stretched and stretched
to nourish and grow two babies at once
in its pocket of love.

milked dry
and left fallow—
its two bulbs extinguished, flickered out.

wrinkly, soft and worn,
an old stuffed animal,
perfect for holding on cold, winter nights.

# Ode to My Breasts

Little buds at first. Nothing much,
until they grew into
bulls eye targets
that stood out,
made me stand out,
to boys who chased me
shouting "get her boobies!"
to men whose stares weighed me down.

But they transformed into magical
milk making machines overnight.
Overnights,
they could calm in an instant,
put two crying babies to sleep at once.
A part of me but hardly mine anymore,
they swelled and gushed with the faintest of cries
and sewed with threads of milk
a timeless mother-child bond.

Their glory days behind them,
they hang like medals.

# Natural Highlights

When I had few,
I'd pluck them out like weeds.
When I could no longer,
I dyed them.
When I tired of dying them,
I succumbed to them,
let them grow unchecked,
their gray heads erupted below a fake sea of black—
slivers of silver scintillating in moonlight.

# Homeless Village

And there it was.
Tucked under an edge
of the Charles River Bridge,
lit by early morning light.

With their colorful tents—
piles of empty tin cans,
like bullet casings,
in rusting supermarket carts
waiting to be redeemed
for a few life-saving dollars,
salvaged mattresses
with their insides protruding,
cracked vodka bottles
spilling out a temporary paradise.

I stare at men emerging
from their staked down tents,
their arms yawning in the morning sun.

I wish I could give them my coat,
the money in my pocket,
my energy bar,
my energy to help them breathe
into another morning.

## Lost Luggage

It didn't make it home with me
more than two decades ago
when I was studying abroad in Israel.

It held summer clothing
my 21-year-old body fit into,
letters from my parents,
my journal, and heirloom coins
mom gave me from her time in Egypt.

I dreamt it was in a dusty lost and found
in a basement closet
with other forgotten suitcases,
lined up like dominoes
or headstones—
time capsules waiting to be claimed.

Perhaps it was found
by a female student
who has a new wardrobe
or a maintenance worker
struggling to make ends meet
who now has clothing for his daughters.

Perhaps it was thrown out,
buried in a dump
under mountains of smelly trash.

I dreamt someone was unpacking it,
reading my parents letters,
fingering my mom's coins,
touching my underwear,
reading my journal,
laying each item on a black table
as if performing an autopsy.

Dust from the slashed suitcase
swirled in the air like ashes.
I shivered in the cold,
so naked you could see my bones.

# Lucid Dreaming

Let me back in again.
I'll stay asleep,
let you play out as you should,
unfurl your raw self like a sapling
in the fertile field of my mind.

So I can somersault in the clouds again,
weightless, like a dandelion seed,
leap from roof tops to the stars,
slide down the crescent moon
into silvery darkness.

Let me back in again,
and then open yourself
to me like a waiting lover,
cocoon me in your invisible net,
mesmerized and paralyzed,
drunk with the illusion
of freedom in my wildest dreams.

# My Hollow

I've been swallowed,
trapped inside a hole,
so long my eyes have adjusted to darkness—
the world seen
through grimy gray.

When the first wavy crack of light
shines through,
a sliver,
a splinter—
my prison revealed.

I try to reach
that one weak crack of light
before it fades,
until the next one pierces through
like a blade, stronger this time,
bright like lightening,
the dark recedes.
I try to climb out,
fall back to rock bottom.

I try to climb out again,
one careful step at a time,
confront darkness
with my head held high,
feel through it
for hand and foot holds,
to lift myself up
into the warm light
of my past life.

# Her Painted Smile

The housewife who endlessly
cooks, cleans, launders, and chauffeurs with a smile—
juggling like a clown to please all
retreats backstage
to a room with clown ceramics, pictures, and bedding.

She searches for her perfect reflection
in the eyes of what resides
behind her frozen, painted, smile.

# Saving a Life

One minute she was
in the back seat with me,
a quiet, shy four-year-old,
the next she hung slack
like a wad of pulled taffy,
inches over the street,
the door swung open,
a gaping mouth—
hers silent.

I lifted her limp body into the moving car
and slammed the door shut,
against the heavy air pressure,
the raging traffic,
the face of death,
we saw in the asphalt's
passing shadows,
and our naked
      fear
that hung
like car exhaust in the air
and aged me far beyond
my twelve sheltered years.

## Ever Since That Day He's Been Carrying Her

The day her eighteen-year-old body
was pulled out of a marsh.

The day he identified his daughter,
the sparkle in her jade eyes extinguished.

The day her blossoming future was stolen,
college, career, marriage, kids—
all of it—
gone in a terrifying moment,
cutoff like a grand opening ribbon,
glittering on the ground.

Some days her body feels light,
as if filled with angel wing feathers.
On others he struggles to breathe
under its pressing weight.

Yet every breath he takes is for her—
to keep her sacred memory alive
and educate others
so they don't suffer the same senseless fate
of murder-by-ex-boyfriend
because it's what she would want—

if the mute body he carries could speak.

# Women's College Reunion

We talk about our aging parents—
arthritis, osteoporosis, knee replacements,
stroke, and Parkinson's.
I imagine our children—
carried by us into this world—
carrying the weight of our aging bodies,
burdened by their dead grandparents,
generations carrying generations
shrouded in veils of our former selves.

# Pears in the Snack Bowl

They put them out right before lunch
next to the chips, granola bars, and nuts—
green speckled pears.
I hover, wait for them like a prayer.

When they are placed in the steel bowl,
I come in for the grab,
stroke its shinny skin and wonder . . .

Who picked it? Was it a migrant worker
struggling to make ends meet for her family?
Was it a farm boy helping his parents?
An elderly farmer with shaky hands
working his last days before retirement?

I sink my teeth into its wonderfully firm, tart flesh.
A few minutes later, I'm staring at its boney core
thinking of my dead father who loved to eat
rock-hard green pears.
The pear doesn't fall far from the tree
even when picked, its roots gone.

# My Granddaughter Sits on My Lap

Generations stare back at me
in her eyes shaped like almonds exactly like
her mother's, her father's, her grandfather's.
Yes, she has my eyelashes,
in their sweeping arc
lies the history of our people.

I grip her tiny hand
dirtied with streaks of colorful marker,
marvel at its softness,
its sponginess—
so foreign to my hard elephant's skin
mapped with many years.

She sits on my well-worn lap,
my legs ache with her weight,
with every soft, giggly, bounce of her.
Her mother sat on it too,
when I was younger,
with my original knees and tree trunk legs.

She smiles at me and I smile back
knowing she'll stand over my grave someday
with strong legs, almond eyes,
more journeys ahead than behind.

# Their Music

He stopped playing when she died.
The piano trapped in a white dusty sheet,
a dead body waiting for the morgue.

His fingers ached for the feel
of the slippery keys,
extensions of his long fingers.

She came to him in a dream,
danced again as he played,
her long, nimble legs threaded
the air like sewing needles,
the music's current
coursed through her
like a second heartbeat.

The last song she danced to played
over and over again
in his mind for years,
hibernated in his finger tips,
like a caged bird longing for release.

He pulled the sheet off,
clouds of dust swirled
like clusters of insects in the sunlight.

As he played,
the notes surged
through him like electricity.

And her ghost performed in front of him,
her movements flowed like water,
like the rain that fell from his eyes,
in a sea of sound.

## Her Volcano

Spring tastes like lemons,
and bird chirps look purple—
synesthesia—
inflamed her path to neuroscience.

She creates cliff-hugging trails
in her Parkinson's Disease research
to find its early mental markers and stem
its neural devastation.

She wants to be the disruption,
the volcano erupting,
cracking the male body of science
and burning roads for the underrepresented.

Underrepresented in research itself,
performed mostly on male mice
and retrofitted
like an ugly burlap sack dress to women.
But she researches both
and writes in capital letters when presenting
"MALE AND FEMALE MICE BOTH."

She's a binder, a combiner
seeking unity where others see difference.
Asked about her ethnicity, "It shouldn't matter.
Our shared experience, what makes us
human at our core, does."

For her, obstacles just aren't.
Her explosive volcano
hurls a fiery, sticky lava.

# Makinde's Quantum World

He believes physics is about understanding our world—
broken and fractured
under the gravity of the eternal.

An everyday world
wildly weird at the
        quantum level,
where he studies systems,
Alice in Wonderland topsy-turvy worlds—
        entangled,
like silky strands of a spider's web,
woven tightly into our lives by our weaving eyes
woven loosely by what we do not see.

        Tangled
with the air touched then tangled
with skin brushed then tangled
with the apple touched at the supermarket then tangled
with the tear wiped then woven away,
tanged with even things very distant like Mars dust,
that unravel themselves
when touched by our gaze—
reveal their hidden essence—
like a string pulled to unwind a knot.

Footprints of the infinite sparkle
in this teeny tiny quantum world
where he tracks God and unravels
delicate threads of the hidden divine.

# About the Author

Miriam Manglani lives in Cambridge, Massachusetts with her husband and three children. She graduated with a degree in English from Brandeis University and a Masters of Education from Harvard University. She works full-time as a Technical Training Manager.

Her poems have been published in various magazines and journals, including *Sparks of Calliope, Red Eft Review, One Art, Glacial Hills Review,* and *Paterson Literary Review.* Her poem "They've Come" was a finalist for the Beals Prize for Poetry. Her poetry chapbook, *Ordinary Wonders,* was published by Prolific Press in 2022.

Visit her online at:
www.miriammanglani.com

www.ingramcontent.com/pod-product-compliance
Lightning Source LLC
Chambersburg PA
CBHW070937160426
43193CB00011B/1720